Collective Biographies

WOMEN IN AMERICA'S WARS

Silvia Anne Sheafer

ENSLOW PUBLISHERS, INC.

44 Fadem Road
Box 699
Springfield, N.J. 07081
U.S.A.

P.O. Box 38
Aldershot
Hants GU12 6BP
U.K.

Library of Congress Cataloging-in-Publication Data

Sheafer, Silvia Anne.
    Women in America's wars / Silvia Anne Sheafer.
       p. cm. — (Collective biographies)
    Includes bibliographical references and index.
    Summary: A collection of ten biographies of women who have served in the
military when America was at war, including Molly Pitcher, Sarah Emma
Edmonds, and Megan Jans.
    ISBN 0-89490-553-8
    1. United States—History, Military—Juvenile literature. 2. United
States—Armed Forces—Women—Biography—Juvenile literature. 3. Women
and war—United States—History—Juvenile literature. 4. Women and the
military—United States—History—Juvenile literature. [1. Women and the
military—History. 2. Women and war—History. 3. United States—History,
Military.]
    I. Title. II. Series.
    E181.S49 1995
    355'.0092'273—dc20
    [B]   95-15473
                                                CIP
                                                AC

Printed in the U.S.A.

10 9 8 7 6 5 4 3 2 1

Illustration Credits:
AP/ Wide World Photos, pp. 68, 76; Courtesy of Lou Ferenz, pp. 58, 65;
Courtesy of Mary Walsh, pp. 78, 85; Courtesy of Megan Jans, pp. 88, 95;
Courtesy of Pamela Davis Dorman, pp. 98, 104; Library of Congress, pp. 8,
35, 48, 55; Monmouth County Historical Association, p. 15; Old Fort
Genealogical Society, Fort Scott, Kansas, pp. 18, 26; Oswego County
Historical Society, p. 28; United States Army Nurse Corps, p. 43; United
States Military Archives, p. 38.

Cover Illustration:
Office of Public Affairs, United States Army

Contents

Preface

Throughout history, American women have endured physical discomfort, personal criticism, and little recognition. They have placed themselves in danger's path— offering their abilities and strengths to preserve values and ensure freedom. Women stood side by side with fathers, husbands, and sons to nurse and comfort the suffering; engage in the danger of spying; chronicle the pain of war; offer spiritual healing; and bear arms. Such women entered the war arena as girls, assumed the jobs of professionals, and performed as heroines. Some women, such as nurse Florence Blanchfield and helicopter pilot Lieutenant Colonel Megan Jans—in the course of time—even earned their own commands.

During World War I, while serving as a nurse in France, Blanchfield found a hospital overburdened with wounded soldiers and lack of medical leadership. She immediately went to work—not only to aid in healing the injured, but to improve the welfare of women nurses. Remaining with the Army through World War II, Blanchfield became chief of the Army Nurse Corps.

Megan Jans was one of the first women helicopter pilots to serve in the Persian Gulf War. In her chosen field she performed duties equal to those of her male counterparts. Jans lead a ground convoy of over four hundred vehicles into the combat zone and flew supplies inside enemy territory.

Lou Ferenz, a flight nurse during World War II, was in charge of transporting wounded soldiers from battle areas in the South Pacific to hospitals in Hawaii. At the war's end she took part in the medical transport of American prisoners of war.

Mary Walsh bears the emotional scars of one of the fiercest hours of the Vietnam conflict. As a physical therapist, and not one to surrender in the face of emotional pain, she cared for severe burn victims and multiple amputees.

Mary Walker was appointed an assistant surgeon during the Civil War—the only woman so employed. While serving in the Union Army, she was captured by Confederate soldiers and imprisoned. After her release she championed the cause of women's rights.

The excitement of reporting world news took Maggie Higgins from college to the battlefronts of Europe and Asia. As a war correspondent, she covered three wars, wrote several books about her war experiences, and received the Pulitzer Prize for international reporting.

Margaret Bourke-White was also a war correspondent. She worked for *Life* magazine as a photographer. Bourke-White covered two wars and was granted interviews with world-famous political figures such as Winston Churchill, Joseph Stalin, and Mohandas Gandhi.

Being a woman made Lieutenant Pamela Davis rare among Navy chaplains. Soon she was called upon to minister on a foreign battlefield. Sent to the Middle East during the Persian Gulf War, Davis performed interdenominational rites for the military.

One of America's most popular heroines is Mary Ludwig Hays McCauley, known as "Molly Pitcher." A soldier's wife during the American Revolution, she followed her husband during battle, carrying water to the soldiers. When her husband fell ill beside his cannon, she took up his position, swabbing and loading the weapon until dawn.

Sarah Emma Edmonds encompassed a wide range of military services—nurse, soldier, and spy. Since women were not eligible as soldiers during the Civil War, Edmonds disguised herself as a man so that she could bear arms. To spy on the Confederate forces, Edmonds used unique disguises as both men and women.

Women such as Ferenz, McCauley, Walsh, Davis, and Edmonds returned home never to see active military duty again. Yet they still ventured beyond the usual roles of women. Some guarded against future wars while some encouraged other women in their endeavors. Both Blanchfield and Jans remained in the military to further the cause of women in service.

Despite working tirelessly, and often above and beyond the call of duty, all these women drew criticism for their efforts. They were criticized because they were treading in an area previously ruled by men. Sometimes these women were not fully honored until many years after their accomplishments—and sometimes only after their deaths. Many women remain unsung and forgotten heroines of important American battles. Their personal and patriotic sacrifices lay silent in the records of historical societies and libaries.

At the end of World War II there were 57,000 Army nurses. In the 12 years of the Vietnam War, 250,000 women also served their country. Profiles of such active women enhance historical events. The profiles also offer a broader understanding of women's significant contributions and the ugly consequences of war.

The remarkable women profiled here offer merely a brief moment in America's long history. Through their example, bravery, intelligence, and wisdom, these women changed the military. They also made lasting impressions on their times, leaving a legacy of valor and patriotism. As women, their service to their country has never been fully honored. Yet, by serving in various positions during war, these women forged new frontiers for future generations. There will always be hurdles to jump and mountains to climb. But such challenges can be better met, thanks to these inspirational examples. In fact, many people can be inspired by the courageous and healing acts of these women.

Mary Hays (center), as depicted in this painting of the Battle of
Monmouth in New Jersey.

Mary Hays
(1754–1832)

On the eve of June 27, 1778, a memorable battle of the American Revolution was about to take place. And Mary Hays, age twenty-four, was to become known as the American heroine "Molly Pitcher." *Molly* was a nickname for Mary, and *Pitcher* was added by thirsty soldiers asking for a pitcher of water.[1]

The British army, under the command of Sir Henry Clinton, had left Philadelphia to retreat across New Jersey. General George Washington, with 8,000 men, followed in the rear. He planned to attack the enemy's left wing. General Charles Lee, with a force of more than 4,000 troops, was sent by Washington to engage Clinton until George Washington arrived.

Lee ordered an attack, but the assault was mismanaged. Soon his army was thrown into confusion, and a retreat was begun. When Washington arrived he took command, rallied the forces, and renewed the assault. The American forces caught up with the British in the next county.

Washington's troops were camped near the town of Freehold in Monmouth County, New Jersey. They were stationed on a hill overlooking the Clinton encampment below. At noon the following day, General Washington ordered his gunners to drive out the British. Their cannons must not stop firing until the enemy retreated. On both sides, every soldier fought to win.[2]

At this time, many soldier's wives traveled with the army from camp to camp. Mary Hays, too, stayed with her husband, John. They had spent a hard winter at Valley Forge, where food was meager and firewood was scarce. But by June the weather was hot. Mary Hays marched alongside the determined young American colonists. The soldiers were a ragged bunch. Some were barefoot, poor, and clad in old clothes. Carrying muskets and long rifles, they were all fighting to be free of Great Britain.

John Hays was a gunner. His job was to fire one of the huge cannons that was pulled from battle to battle. When a ball was fired, hot gases poured from the cannon's barrel. The metal ramrod used to push the cannon ball into the breech also became very hot.

Despite the heat, the battle began. At noon the temperature neared 100°F. Hundreds of soldiers, exhausted from the heat, fell on the ground next to the dead. Mary Hays grabbed a pitcher, filling it with water from a nearby stream. She raced across the battlefield from one soldier to another, offering each water. "Let me give you a drink," she said. "I'll hold up your head. Come, now, drink from my pitcher."[3]

The battle-weary soldiers accepted the water, drinking until the pitcher was empty. Hays returned to the stream, filling the pitcher again and again. With feeble voices the sick men called her. "Molly! Molly! Pitcher! Pitcher!" Sometimes these calls were just "Molly Pitcher, Molly Pitcher." Others who heard the call thought that this was the woman's name. So they too called for Molly Pitcher.[4]

Throughout the battle, Hays continued to bring water to the fallen men. Suddenly she caught sight of John. He was sagging from exhaustion, hanging over the cannon. As Mary rushed to his side she saw him fall. He was not wounded, but overcome by the heat of the cannon and the sweltering sun. Mary cradled John in her arms. She soaked a rag in the cold water from her pitcher and tied it around his head. Gently she moved him away from the cannon. He could not be revived.

General Washington had said that the cannons must not be silenced. An orderly came running. "Why is this gun silent? Where is the gunner?"

Hays pointed to her strickened husband. "He can't fire another shot. He is exhausted."

11

"Is there no other gunner here?"[5]

Hays grabbed the ramrod. "I'll fire it!" she cried. "I've watched my husband. I know I can swab and load."[6]

As the bullets fell around Hays she swabbed, loaded, and fired the huge cannon. Her face and clothes became blackened from gunpowder.[7] The sun beat down upon her. She fired the cannon until darkness silenced the guns. Stretcher-bearers came for the wounded. John Hays was carried to a field hospital. The Battle of Monmouth was finally over.

Believing that the battle would continue at daybreak, Mary Hays stayed by the cannon. However, when the sun began to creep upon the horizon, the British were gone. They had fled during the night. The Americans lost 230 wounded or killed. The British lost 249.

Mary Ludwig Hays was born near Trenton, New Jersey, in 1754. She was the daughter of John and Gretchen Ludwig. Her mother was Dutch and her father, German. Her parents traveled with other relatives to the American colonies before Mary was born. Most of their kin lived near Mary's father's dairy farm.

Mary grew up on the farm with her younger brothers Kurt and Carl. Like other children of the colonial times, she fed the chickens, made cheese and hoecakes (a cake made of Indian meal baked before a fire on a hoe), cooked meals, and raised her own calf.

Eventually hard times struck the valley. People did not have enough money to pay the last tax King George III of England had demanded for the French and Indian War of 1763. Mary soon learned about the British from the other farmers. They levied unfair taxes on the colonists. Taxation without representation is tyranny.[8] The colonists had come to America to escape tyranny and persecution. In the mid-eighteenth century the British Parliament passed a series of tough laws. The British stationed troops among the colonists, regulated trade, and closed American frontiers to settlement. Revolution was brewing among the settlers. Soon the thirteen American colonies revolted.

Early in the war Mary's older brothers left to fight the British. Joshua Ludwig went to be a sailor and Joseph Ludwig, a soldier. In 1766, when Mary was about twelve, she moved to Carlisle, Pennsylvania, to work as a servant in the home of Colonel William Irvine. Irvine was a doctor who treated the farmers and the soldiers. In 1769, when Mary was fifteen, she returned to her parents' home and married John Casper Hays, a young barber who lived in Carlisle.

General George Washington assumed command of the Continental Army in July 1775. On July 4, 1776, Congress adopted the Declaration of Independence. The colonists had declared their independence. Now they had to fight for it. This meant defeating Great Britain, which had the greatest naval power in the world. British armies too, at one time or another, defeated every important country in Europe.

During 1777, regiments of American soldiers often passed the Ludwig dairy farm. They were going east to fight the British soldiers. They were part of General George Washington's band of patriots who had eagerly volunteered. When the soldiers passed, Mary Hays told them that she was a patriot too and so were her mother and father.

John Hays enlisted as a gunner in the First Pennsylvania artillery. During the winters of 1777 and 1778 he was stationed at Valley Forge. General Washington had taken his troops there after they were defeated at Philadelphia and Germantown, Pennsylvania. The winter was a bitter test of loyalty for the American soldiers. They had little food and hardly enough clothing to protect themselves. The army of about 10,000 lived in crude huts, which the soldiers had built themselves. Two days before Christmas George Washington wrote: "We have this day no less than 2,873 men in camp unfit for duty because they are barefooted and otherwise naked."[9]

The period of Valley Forge, often described as "the Winter of Despair," was one of the most difficult times of the war.[10] Mary Hays, however, remained in camp with her husband and made herself useful by cooking, washing, and doing other work. Despite the suffering, the general and his troops stayed in Valley Forge throughout the winter and spring. In

General George Washington (depicted on horseback) personally thanked Mary Hays for the courage she displayed at the Battle of Monmouth.

June General Washington was able to move his army against the British.

That summer, after the Battle of Monmouth when Mary Hays fired the cannon, she became an American legend. General Washington invited her to his headquarters. He congratulated her for the courage she showed during the battle and for staying at the cannon.

At Monmouth the Americans had dealt the British army a heavy blow. General Washington thanked Hays for her help and made her a sergeant in the army. He pinned a badge of honor on her too.

Mary Hays received a salute and a loud cheer from the soldiers. The other generals—Henry Knox, Nathaniel Greene, and French General Marquis de Lafayette—also commended her. General Lafayette asked her to review his troops. Mary Hays walked between the two lines of French soldiers, and they all saluted her.

When the war ended in 1783 Mary and John Hays returned to Carlisle, Pennsylvania. Several years after John Hays' death in 1789, Mary Hays married George McCauley. He too had been a soldier in the American Revolution and a friend of her late husband. But the marriage proved an unhappy union.

Military pensions are granted to war veterans and their dependents. They are the oldest form of pensions granted by the United States government. The first general military-pension law was passed in 1792 to aid veterans of the American Revolution. At first, pensions were granted only to disabled veterans. But in 1818, the first pension based on service was adopted by Congress. Pensions were not granted to widows of men who fought in the American Revolution until 1836. The American Revolution cost the government about $70 million in pensions.

Individual states, such as Pennsylvania where Mary Hays McCauley lived, eventually gave pensions too. However, those provided were generally smaller and for specific endeavors.

In 1822, Mary Hays McCauley was awarded a yearly pension of $40 by the state legislature of Pennsylvania.[11]

Sarah Emma Edmonds

Sarah Emma Edmonds

(1841–1898)

During her life Sarah Emma Evelyn Edmonds was a nurse, soldier, and Union Army spy. In the summer of 1862 she had spying on her mind. General George B. McClellan, leading 53,000 Union troops, was preparing to battle the Confederate forces of General John B. Magruder, who was holding Yorktown, Virginia. Only the previous summer had the Union Army planned to march on Richmond, Virginia, and end the Civil War. But the Confederate Army proved stronger than expected.

In 1862 Edmonds suffered the loss of the young soldier with whom she was deeply in love.[1] She had been serving as a nurse, tending the battlefield wounded and dying. Her lover was killed by a Confederate sharpshooter during the second battle of

Bull Run on August 30. Since that day she was no longer content to serve only as a nurse. She became a spy, gathering vital information for the Union Army about activities of the Confederate forces.

Her first act of espionage involved donning a double disguise—both in race and gender. For three days she prepared for the transformation. First she bought a suit of work clothes much like those worn by African-American slaves who labored in the cotton and tobacco fields. Next she had a barber cut her hair short and close to the scalp. Finally she bought burnt cork to blacken her face, hands, and arms.

Her biggest obstacle was acquiring a black wig. With her face blackened, she approached a mail boat preparing to leave for Washington, D.C. She asked the postmaster to buy her a "black" wig. When questioned about such a purchase, she told him that it was "for some 'noiterin' business."[2]

When the boat returned, carrying her black wig, Edmonds' disguise as an African-American boy was complete. She returned to General McClellan's encampment. There, she gathered some crackers, a loaded pistol, and set out for the Confederate camp.

Near midnight she reached her destination. She lay down to rest on a bed of leaves. The next morning Edmonds was awakened by African-American slaves bringing breakfast to the pickets on guard. She made their acquaintance, and when they returned she followed them inside the Confederate fortifications.

"Who do you belong to and why are you not at work?" demanded an officer.

The officer turned to another soldier, telling him to put the "black rascal . . . to work. . . . there are no free [blacks] here!"[3]

All day Edmonds pushed a wheelbarrow filled with gravel. At nightfall, despite fatigue and blistered hands, she roamed about the camp, taking notes. She counted the number of soldiers and wrote down the size of the cannon. She also roughly sketched the outer works of the camp.

The following day she changed places with another slave, supplying drinking water to the troops. She managed to gather information about the arrival of General Joseph E. Johnston and the number of reinforcements expected. The most staggering information was that Confederate forces would secretly leave Yorktown and retreat toward Richmond. On the third night of her spying she quietly slipped through the picket lines, bringing back the information to General McClellan. This information helped the Union general plan his attack.

During the Civil War female espionage increased in numbers previously unmatched. With husbands, sons, and fathers already in battle and with the desire to make some contribution to this great struggle, women sought tidbits that they considered valuable to the cause. "The ladies were terrific. In this war they made their debut in American espionage."[4]

In their enthusiasm and inexperience with war, the women deluged Union and Confederate headquarters alike with outpourings of gossip and trivia. Some of the women went so far as to masquerade as men. They succeeded in enlisting and wearing the military uniforms of the Blue and the Gray. Sarah Emma Edmonds was one of these women.

Sarah Edmonds was born in December 1841 in New Brunswick, Canada. She received little education as a child. Sometime in the 1850s she ran away from home. In 1859, after a brief reunion with her mother and family, she hiked all the way to Hartford, Connecticut. Edmonds had a religious fervor and an adventurous spirit. She had learned to carry a gun and was a good shot. For a time she worked as a Bible salesperson, dressing as a man and assuming the name of Frank Thompson.

Working her way west Edmonds arrived in Flint, Michigan, in 1861. When the Civil War broke out in April 1861 she enlisted in the Union Army. As "Frank Thompson" she became a soldier in a volunteer infantry company that became Company F, 2nd Michigan Infantry. For nearly a year her disguise was a success. In most regiments women were not allowed to be soldiers. They really had to look like a man to be enlisted.

As "Frank Thompson," Edmonds took part in the battles of Blackburn's Ford and the first Bull Run in the peninsular campaign of May through July 1862. As "Frank Thompson" again, Edmonds served as an aide to Colonel Orlando M. Poe at Fredericksburg, Virginia, in December 1862. There, she witnessed the humiliating defeat that cost the Union 12,700 men. The Confederate Army sustained 5,300 dead.[5]

After Edmonds became a spy she developed several masquarades. For her second mission she appeared as an Irish-American female peddler of baked goods. Edmonds dressed up as an Irish peasant woman, wore eyeglasses, carried an arm basket, and peddled cakes and pies. She also brushed up on common Irish phrases. Then she acquired a horse and set off in the direction of the Confederate camp near Chickahominy, Virginia.

That night, wet from having to forge the Chickahominy swamp, Edmonds was attacked by chills and delirium, "tortured by fiends of every conceivable shape and magnitude."[6] Her horse had long since returned to its camp.

At dawn the roar of cannons and shells crashing through the swamp awakened her. Trudging through the wooded area she stumbled upon a cottage. Inside she discovered a Confederate soldier. Allen Hull was gravely ill with typhoid fever and had had no nourishment since leaving camp. Hull said to Edmonds, "Keep this ring in memory of one whose suffering you have alleviated and whose soul has been refreshed by your prayers in the hour of dissolution."

Edmonds made the dying man some tea and prayed with him. His last request was that she take his gold watch and a packet of letters to Major McKee of General Richard Ewell's staff. What better way for Edmonds to penetrate the enemy lines then as a personal favor to a dying Confederate soldier. With a humanity mission and a convincing Irish brogue, she easily passed the Confederate picket guard.

Then she overheard the guard report that one of their spies had just returned from the field. The spy said that the Yankees had finished the bridge across the Chickahominy River and intended to attack, either today or tonight. But Jackson and Lee were ready for them. The Confederates had masked batteries along all parts of the road.[7]

Realizing the importance of the guard's remarks, Edmonds knew that she had to get back to the Union camp. Yet, first she must fulfill her promise to the dying Confederate and deliver his gold watch and letters to Major McKee.

So overcome with her good intentions, McKee ordered a horse for Edmonds. Together, with a detachment of twenty-four Confederate soldiers, they rode to retrieve the remains of the dead soldier.

When Edmonds was requested to ride down the road and watch for the Union Army, her opportunity was at hand. Slowly she rode down the road into the approaching darkness. After a safe distance she turned the horse into a gallop, racing for the Union lines on the Chickahominy. Edmonds knew that she was betraying the confidence that had been placed in her by the dying soldier. But she also had a duty to get important information back to the Union camp. She presented the vital information while the Confederates were bringing back the body of the dead soldier.

Later, again as "Frank Thompson," she accompanied the 2nd Michigan to Kentucky. In April 1863 she contracted malaria (a disease, transmitted by the bite of a mosquito, causing high fever and chills). Fearing her deception would be revealed in an Army hospital, she deserted.[8]

Using her own name of Sarah Edmonds, she next worked as a nurse for the U.S. Christian Commission. In 1865, after the end of the war, she published a popular fictionalized account of her experiences called *Nurse and Spy in the Union Army.* It sold 175,000 copies. She donated her share of the profits to war relief.

Edmonds married Linus Seelye on April 27, 1867. They had three children—all of whom died before reaching adulthood. They also adopted two sons, George Frederick, born in 1872, and Charles Finney Seelye, born in 1874. Later she and her husband moved from Kansas, to Ohio, to Michigan, and finally, to Texas to be nearer an adopted son and his family.

Before leaving Kansas, Edmonds began securing affidavits from old Army comrades in order to apply for a veteran's pension. In July 1884 Congress granted the pension to Sarah E. E. Seeyle, alias Frank Thompson. A short time before her death in 1898, Edmonds became the only Texan woman to

Shortly after the war ended, Sarah Edmonds published a fictionalized account of her adventures called *Nurse and Spy in the Union Army.*

be mustered into the Grand Army of the Republic as a regular member.

Edmonds was initially buried at La Porte, Texas; but in 1901, her body was reburied in the G.A.R. (Grand Army of the Republic) part of the Washington Cemetery in Houston. In July 1988 Sarah Edmonds Seeyle was inducted into the Military Intelligence Corps Hall of Fame at Fort Huachuca, Arizona.

Mary Edwards Walker

3

Mary Edwards Walker

(1832–1919)

In September 1863 General William Rosecrans and his Union Army of the Cumberland were moving into Alabama toward Chattanooga, Tennessee. General Braxton Bragg and his Confederate Army of Tennessee were ready to counterattack. The Civil War was now in its twenty-ninth month. The Union realized that—despite recent victories at Gettysburg, Pennsylvania, and Vicksburg, Mississippi—the war was not near an end. The Confederates took comfort in the fact that—despite defeats in Pennsylvania and on the Mississippi—they were still afloat and fighting.

That summer was also a month of personal achievement for Mary Edwards Walker. Becoming a doctor had not been easy for Walker. While women were commonly recognized as nurses, few were able to overcome the obstacles of graduating from a medical school. The practice of medicine in the mid-1800s was a man's profession. But Walker had been determined to succeed in that profession. A Virginian sympathetic to the Union cause, General George H. Thomas was named to his post by President Abraham Lincoln in 1861. In 1862 General Thomas appointed Mary Walker assistant surgeon in the Army of the Cumberland. No honor for a professional woman could have been greater. Not only had the Army recognized her as a doctor, but she was also the only woman so engaged in the Civil War.

The summer was hot in the gently rolling country-side of Tennessee. Wooded near the river, the ground inland was covered with dry scrub brush. Clouds of dust from the many small battles clogged fields and roads. The dust mingled with the early morning fog that rose off the Tennessee River. General Thomas was engaged in skirmishes and battles near Chattanooga and Chickamauga, Georgia. He assigned Walker to the 52nd Ohio Regiment with the rank of first lieutenant in the Union Army. She quickly adopted the standard officers' uniform, suitably modifying it to her figure. With her commission Congress had granted her permission to wear men's attire. At that time there were no regulation uniforms for women.

The field hospitals were tents erected at the rear of the battlelines. Often they were inadequate to house the hundreds of soldiers who were wounded, diseased, and dying of starvation. With little medicine Walker worked tirelessly to lessen their suffering.

Mary Edwards Walker was born on a farm near Oswego, New York, on November 26, 1832. Her father was a school teacher. After early schooling she went on to study medicine at Syracuse Medical College. In 1855 she graduated and received her M.D. Walker's medical graduation was a significant accomplishment because even nursing schools for women were few.

After graduation Walker established a practice in Rome, New York. That same year she married Albert Miller. Miller was a doctor with whom she practiced. But the marriage did not last, and the couple was separated in 1859. Ten years later Walker and Miller were finally officially divorced.

From an early age Mary Walker had been interested in changing styles of dress for women. She said that corsets (the stiff undergarments worn by women of that era) were "coffins."[1] She became an ardent follower of Amelia Bloomer, another dress reformer and an advocate of women's rights. Bloomer was a popular figure in the late 1850s, making speeches and appearing in public wearing full-cut pantaloons, or "Turkish trousers," dubbed "bloomers." It is unclear whether or not Mary Walker ever met Amelia Bloomer. But Walker was interested in what Bloomer was advocating—women's rights and related dress reforms for women, including loose pants and jackets.

At the outbreak of the Civil War in 1861, Walker had traveled to Washington, D.C., to offer her services. She first worked as a volunteer nurse in the Patient Office Hospital. Meanwhile, she attempted to gain a regular appointment to the Army medical service. At this time women were sometimes serving the Army as nurses and matrons (widowed women supervising other women and caring for the wounded)—but not as doctors.

Not having any luck in her quest, Walker left Washington, D.C., from January to February 1862 to attend the New York Hygeio-Therapeutic College. In that same year she began working in the field. And in September General Thomas finally appointed her assistant surgeon with the 52nd Ohio Regiment.

Mary Walker cared for the wounded until 1863 when she was captured by the Confederate Army in Chattanooga. Seven months later, in April 1864, she was imprisoned in Castle Thunder (a converted tobacco warehouse) in Richmond, Virginia. In August she was exchanged for a Confederate officer of her own rank.

Following her release Walker was given a contract as "acting assistant surgeon," but saw no more field service. The war ended in April 1865, and Walker was assigned for the next two months to a women's prison hospital and then to an orphanage. She left government service in June 1865. A short time later, by order of President Andrew Johnson, she was awarded the Medal of Honor (now called the Congressional Medal of Honor).

When the war ended, Walker went to Europe. She was given audiences with kings and queens and praised for her war-work accomplishments. In 1866 Mary Walker was elected president of the National Dress Reform Association. At this time she was a friend of another feminist reformer, Belva A. Lockwood. Lockwood, a teacher, had sought to enter law school. However, she was refused admission to Columbian College (now George Washington University), Georgetown University, and Howard University. She later studied law at the National University Law School, and was admitted to the bar in 1873. In 1879 she won passage of a measure that allowed women lawyers to practice before the U.S. Supreme Court.

Walker joined Lockwood in various reform movements, and Walker's Civil War service was widely publicized by feminist organizations. During this period of her life Walker sought to financially assist other women who had served as nurses and matrons during the war. She wrote the following to Benjamin Alvord, acting paymaster of the U.S. Army:

> Please give the names of the women who acted in the capacity of matrons and nurses, and of all the women who were paid by your department for serving during the late war. If possible let me hear from you as early as Friday evening of the present week.[2]

Benjamin Alvord responded:

> There is no mode in which this office can give you the desired information, the rolls upon which such payments were made have passed into the hands of 2nd Auditor of the Treasury.

This matter was never settled. Walker continued to rally for various social changes, including dress reform for women, suffrage for women, prohibition of the manufacture and sale of alcohol, total destruction of tobacco, and uniform divorce laws for the entire United States.[3]

Mary Walker grew increasingly eccentric, wearing men's dress attire—complete with wing collar, bow tie, and top hat. She was often arrested for masquerading as a man. But Walker claimed that she had been granted permission to do so by Congress. However, there is no record of any such action.[4]

The women's suffrage movement continued during this period. Though Walker sought various reforms, she viewed the question of suffrage as pointless. In her opinion, the United States Constitution had already given the vote to women. Therefore, the legislation sought by organized suffragists was needless.[5] (The United States Constitution did not grant full voting rights to women until August 26, 1920.)

Mary Walker is thought to have invented the idea of attaching a postcard receipt to registered mail, a

Mary Edwards Walker would often wear men's dress attire. She was often arrested for masquerading as a man.

practice still carried out today. Walker also attended political meetings, from town caucuses to national conventions, and insisted that she be heard on women's rights. At times she was not given the courtesy of making a speech and she became outraged.[6]

Always controversial, Walker published two books: the partly autobiographical *Hit* released in 1871 and *Unmasked, of the Science of Immortality* released in 1878. Her eccentricity increased, and in 1887 she exhibited herself—wearing men's clothes—in dime museum sideshows.[7]

In 1881 she announced her candidacy for United States senator from New York. Among her qualifications she stated that her "brain had not been numbed by drugs, liquor or tobacco."[8] She was not elected.

Four years later she said that she was a Democrat and claimed the right to vote because she was a citizen and taxpayer. In November 1885 she appeared at the polling place in Oswego Center, demanding that she be given a ballot and allowed to vote. Upon being refused she threatened legal action against the election board.[9]

Considered by most to be generally harmless, Mary Walker lived the remainder of her life in Oswego, New York. She was proud of her Medal of Honor and wore it frequently. Yet in 1917 it was revoked (as were hundreds of others) because there was no record of the occasion of the award. Walker refused to surrender her prized possession.

A fall on the steps of the Capitol building in Washington, D.C., left her infirm. Walker died in Oswego, New York, on February 21, 1919, and was buried at the Old Acre at Rural Cemetery. In 1978, fifty-nine years later, President Jimmy Carter reinstated her Medal of Honor.

Florence Aby Blanchfield

Florence Aby Blanchfield

(1882–1971)

World War I was to be the war to end all wars. Eight million soldiers lost their lives in the greatest struggle the world had so far seen. It began in August 1914. The Austrian crown prince Archduke Francis Ferdinand and his wife were shot on June 28, 1914, by a Serbian nationalist in Sarajevo. Sarajevo was the capital of Bosnia, a province in the Austria-Hungarian Empire. This provided a reason for Austria to attack Serbia. Germany supported Austria and Russia (the Axis powers). Great Britain and France (the Allies) supported Serbia.

Throughout the early part of the war the United States remained neutral. But American manufacturers were sending supplies to Allied Europe. With the use of submarines the Germans attempted to cut off the American flow of arms. They began all-out submarine warfare in 1917. That same year American ships were sunk, and lives and property were lost. On April 6, 1917, the United States declared war on Germany. Two months later the first American Expeditionary Forces landed in France. A deadly conflict ensued.

In October, in accord with the American commitment, Florence Blanchfield assumed duties as an Army staff nurse at Base Hospital No. 27 in Angers, France. Her rank was that of lieutenant. Two months later she was appointed acting chief nurse at Camp Hospital No. 15 in Camp Coetquidan, also in France.

Winter snow and rain made the situation extremely difficult. Ambulances bumped over mud-clogged roads. The air was sickish with the dank smell of campfire smoke and mist rising off the uncovered meadows. Encamped near the hospital was a regiment on the way to the front. The soldiers had built little shelters in the angles of stone walls. A handful of grave-faced men stood around fires, stamping their feet to keep warm.

In the hospital yard, stretcher-bearers unloaded the wounded and dying from Red Cross ambulances. To the north, cannon flashes jabbed the sky. Inside the hospital, housed in an old building, Blanchfield tended the injured. She was a long way from home.[1]

Florence Aby Blanchfield was born on April 1, 1882, in Shepherdstown, West Virginia. She was the second of three daughters, in a family of eight children, born to Mary Anderson Blanchfield and Joseph Plunkett Blanchfield. As a child she attended public school in Walnut Springs, West Virginia, and the Oranda Institute—a private boarding school in Oranda, Virginia.

After high school graduation, Blanchfield traveled to the city of her mother's birth—Pittsburgh, Pennsylvania—and entered the South Side Hospital Training School for Nurses. Her mother had been a nurse and her maternal grandfather and an uncle were doctors. In fact, all three Blanchfield daughters became trained nurses. Blanchfield received her nursing degree in 1906. During a period of private-duty nursing in 1907, she completed a postgraduate course in operating room supervision and technique at John Hopkins Hospital in Baltimore, Maryland. She then returned to Pittsburgh and became operating room supervisor at Montefiore Hospital.

Her nursing abilities were rewarded when she assumed the position as superintendent and director of nursing at Suburban General Hospital in Bellevue, Pennsylvania. Achieving this goal was only the beginning of a distinguished career. A foreign appointment was on the horizon for the young nurse.

In 1903 the United States secured exclusive control of the Panama Canal Zone. The task of building a canal connecting the Atlantic and Pacific Oceans was turned over to the engineers of the U.S. Army. At the peak of construction there were more than

35,000 persons working on the project. Hospital personnel were needed to care for the sick and accident victims. Under a Civil Service appointment in 1913, Blanchfield joined the staff of Ancon Hospital in the Panama Canal Zone.

Apart from job-related injuries, the Americans found Panama to be "one of the hottest, wettest and most feverish regions in existence." Yellow fever, malaria, and the bubonic plague were the greatest handicaps to the completion of the canal.[2] Under the direction of Colonel W. C. Gorgas these deadly diseases were eventually curbed. But for some time they remained significant hospital caseloads. Blanchfield gained further medical knowledge in the treatment of these diseases.

After her Panama duty, Blanchfield briefly worked as an emergency surgical nurse for the U.S. Steel Corporation in Bessemer, Pennsylvania. Between 1915 and 1917, she also found time to complete a course of study at Martin Business College in Pittsburgh.

But it was the nursing during World War I that changed her life. The initial taste of military life was more than enough to convince Blanchfield that she had found a career that was to be hers for the next twenty-seven years. After a brief stint at Suburban General Hospital in August 1917, she donned the uniform of an Army nurse once again. Blanchfield wore the uniform proudly and with great honor. Her goal was to gain full military rank for nurses.

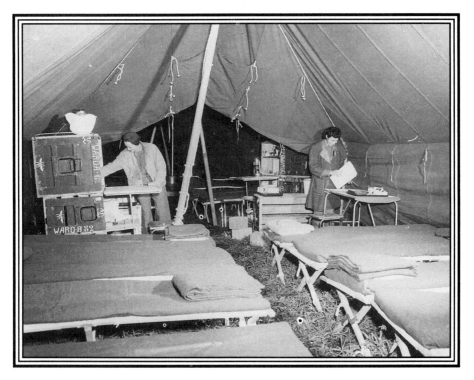

Florence Blanchfield worked as an Army nurse in France during World War I. Here, two nurses prepare a field hospital to receive wounded soldiers.

While stationed at Camp Custer, Michigan, in April 1920, Florence was promoted to chief nurse with the relative rank of first lieutenant. (Relative rank means title without military status, comparable pay, or allowances accruing to fully commissioned officers; it is similar to noncommissioned officer status.)[3] In the next fifteen years Blanchfield held ranking positions at hospitals in Indiana; California; the Philippine Islands; Georgia; Washington, D.C.; and Missouri—ending with a tour in the American hospital in Tientsin, China, in 1935.

Blanchfield next reported to the Office of the Surgeon General. Four years later she was promoted to the relative rank of captain and assumed the position of first assistant to the superintendent of the Army Nurse Corps. She handled assignments, transfers, discharges, records—the types of problems inherent in managing several hundred women in military hospitals around the world.

During Blanchfield's tenure in office the Army Nurse Branch of Technical Information in the Office of the Surgeon General was established. It spread information to civilian organizations that assisted in recruiting nurses to serve with the military forces.

World war once again broke out, and Blanchfield faced another career landmark. Her immediate supervisor, Lieutenant Colonel Julia O. Flikke, had become disabled. An Army committee to study the medical department was requested by the U.S. government. The committee strongly advocated that the Nursing Division of the Army Nurse Corps be reorganized and strengthen.[4] As a result of the committee's investigation, Flikke retired and Blanchfield was named superintendent of the Corps. She was promoted to lieutenant colonel in 1942.

In addition to increasing the efficiency of nursing care of America's sick and wounded soldiers, Blanchfield had a deep and abiding interest in the welfare of all nurses under her command. In pursuit of this interest, she recommended the establishment of basic training centers for newly appointed nurses in the nine continental Service Commands and in all overseas theaters. Another significant change resulted in the assignment of nurses to field and evacuation hospitals near the frontlines in order to provide expert nursing care to battle casualties.[5]

Blanchfield was instrumental in securing full military rank, albeit temporary commissioned status, for Army nurses in 1944. This was brought about by an excellent public relations program that solicited support from key government officials as well as civilian nursing organizations. Blanchfield also made an extended tour of the European Theater of Operations to insure superior care of casualties.

Perhaps even more challenging than the rapid wartime buildup to a strength of over 57,000 army nurses, was the difficult period following World War II—when nearly 50,000 nurses were disbanded. Blanchfield was acutely aware of the need for continuing service for the thousands of wounded, still hospitalized, as well as for the armies of occupation. She strove to improve the working and living conditions of her nurses. Blanchfield succeeded, in large part, because she insisted on being readily accessible to all under her command.

By 1945 Blanchfield had received many accolades. The most prestigious came from the War Department. For "demonstrating outstanding ability and devotion to duty as Superintendent of the Army Nurse Corps and by her precept and example," she was awarded the Distinguished Service Medal:[6]

> She was responsible for policies used in expanding the Corps from a few hundred nurses to more than fifty-two thousand, displaying administrative and executive ability of the highest order. In 1944 she was largely instrumental in securing full military rank for nurses. . . . She planned and put into operation a program which took nursing teams close to the front lines for surgical duty—a new procedure which helped save lives by insuring prompt nursing care. . . . Colonel Blanchfield's wise understanding of nurses and their problems was a major factor in the success of her organization. (Citation for the Distinguished Service Medal).[7]

A few months before her retirement in September 1947, Blanchfield's efforts to obtain permanent commissioned status for military nurses resulted in congressional passage of the Army-Navy Nurse Act of 1947. On July 18 General Dwight D. Eisenhower, then Army Chief of Staff, presented her with the first regular Army commission conferred on a woman in the U.S. Army.

In 1951, topping off her distinguished career, the International American Red Cross presented her with the highest award for which a nurse is eligible—the Florence Nightingale Medal. And in 1963 West Virginia awarded its famous daughter the State Distinguished Service Medal for "bringing honor and distinction as a humanitarian to herself and to her State."

Florence Blanchfield remained active until her death on May 12, 1971—the birthday of Florence Nightingale. She was buried with full military honors in Arlington National Cemetery in Arlington, Virginia.

Margaret Bourke-White

Margaret Bourke-White

(1906–1971)

The flagship shuddered as a German torpedo
pierced its hull, sending a violent rush of seawater
rumbling through its breach. In minutes the ship
went into a sudden sharp list, mortally damaged. Inside one of the staterooms Margaret Bourke-White,
an American photographer/journalist, was cata-
pulted out of her bunk. In the melee she and three
Scottish nursing nuns struggled to their feet.

Holding onto the bunk, Bourke-White hurriedly
dressed. Then, wishing the sisters luck, she threw her
musette bag, containing one camera and several rolls
of film, over her shoulder and dashed out.[1]

In the ship's stairwell she joined the swelling
stream of men and women trying to get topside.
Part of a convoy, the ship was carrying 6,000 British

and American soldiers, nurses, and Womens Army Corps (WACs). The ship was heading for the North African coast and the 1942 Allied invasion of Tunisia.

The deck was listing as the ship began slowly rolling over. The threatening sound of splashing seawater and trampling feet broke the silence. A brilliant moon illuminated the midnight sky. The ship's towering hull dwarfed hundreds of men and women scrambling down the rope nets flung over the ship's side. Far below, the churning Mediterranean was alive with men and women swimming, or hanging onto floating debris, and lifeboats spilling over with panicked people.

Bourke-White hugged the camera to her chest as her assigned lifeboat made its quivering descent. When she had previously asked General Jimmy Doolittle, commanding general of the Eighth Air Force, if she could cover the invasion, Bourke-White assumed that she would fly. Ironically, Doolittle told her that she should be sent by sea in a convoy—the nice safe way.[2]

The lifeboat slammed the water's surface, miraculously drifting away from the suction of the sinking ship. As the light of dawn broke across the distant horizon, the survivors began to cheer. By mid-afternoon Bourke-White caught everyone joyfully waving to an English flying boat.

Photography had helped Bourke-White pay her way through school. One of three children, she was born on June 14, 1906, in New York

City. Her father was an engineer and inventor, building the first press for printing Braille. The whole family enjoyed natural history along with a zest for life. The family's home was always filled with plants and animals. Bourke-White caught that interest with such lasting ardor that it nearly made her a biologist instead of a photographer.

At Plainfield High School in New Jersey she was one of the editors of the high school newspaper. She also loved dancing. Bourke-White enrolled at Columbia University to study art. Then she left for the University of Michigan, becoming a student of herpetology (the study of reptiles). Still undecided about her future she entered Cornell University. She'd "read that there were waterfalls on campus."[3]

Later Bourke-White would say that it was the drama of waterfalls that first gave her the idea that she should put her camera to work.[4] She took up photography, first as a hobby and then on a freelance basis. After graduating from Cornell in 1927, Bourke-White moved to New York City and established herself as an architectural and industrial photographer.

For her professional name she combined her own last name with her mother's maiden name (Bourke) to create the hyphenated form by which she was known thereafter. Taking freelance work across the country, Bourke-White perfected her art. She often used natural light and the cavernous interiors of the Cleveland steel mills and the open-hearth mill of

Ford Motor Company to create striking photographs. For one shot she crawled out on an overhanging steel gargoyle on the sixty-first floor of the Chrysler building to photograph the city below.

Bourke-White's command of the camera brought her increasingly important commissions. She was noticed by Henry Luce, the young publisher of *Time* magazine. He asked her to join him in launching another publication, *Fortune*. Bourke-White's dramatic photos would become partners with words creating a new concept in storytelling for the growing business and industrial markets. From *Fortune*'s founding in 1929 until 1933 Bourke-White was associate editor. Her dramatic black-and-white study of Fort Peck Dam, Montana, was *Fortune*'s first cover illustration. During this time several extensive tours of the then Soviet Union resulted in her publications, *Eyes on Russia*, *Red Republic*, and *U.S.S.R., a Portfolio of Photographs.*

Three years later Luce launched *Life* magazine. A member of the original staff, Bourke-White remained an editor of *Life* for thirty-three years, contributing countless photos and photo-essays.

Bourke-White's first marriage was to Everett Chapman in 1925. They divorced the following year. She married Erskine Caldwell in 1939, and they too were divorced in 1942. Caldwell was an American novelist and short-story writer. He wrote *Tobacco Road* and *God's Little Acre,* novels depicting the poor of rural America. Together, they produced three books: *You Have Seen Their Faces,* a vivid study of the rural South; *North of the Danube,* and *Say! Is This the U.S.A.?*

When the ominous clouds of World War II loomed in 1939, *Life* sent Bourke-White to Europe, the Near East, and the Soviet Union. In 1941 she photographed Josef Stalin as well as Soviet military and political events. There she had her first and lasting view of the German bombing of Moscow. Bourke-White's dedication to photojournalism and her bravery in 1942 would later earn her the title of the first woman to be accredited as a war correspondent for the U.S. Army and *Life* magazine.

After surviving the torpedoing of the convoy ship, Bourke-White arrived in North Africa. There, she moved forward with the troops into Italy. Outside Naples she was stationed in a fourteenth-century monastery. With her assigned jeep and driver, Bourke-White would scout every day for the best stories and where the most action would take place.

In January 1944 the war had reached an agonizing stage. Allied forces were trying to break through the mountains surrounding the Cassino Valley. By now Bourke-White had flown in almost all modes of airships. It was not unusual when she joined a Piper Cub on a scouting mission for a Screaming Meemie—a German eight-barreled rocket gun.

Crossing the hillcrest surrounding the valley, the mountains sharply dropped away. The land was pockmarked with thousands of shell holes, filled with water, shimmering in the early morning sunlight. Twisted bridges, burning brush, and endless smoke clouded the view. "Its been so rough down there," said Captain Marinelli, "that the boys are calling it Purple Heart Valley."[5]

Approaching a stretch of land where the bushes were violently blowing back, Marinelli pointed to the German gun's hidden emplacement. He got on the two-way radio with the Allied artillery gun crew, zeroing them in on target.

Suddenly the air was screaming in their ears. Marinelli was taking the Piper Cub into a steep dive. Over her shoulder Bourke-White caught a glimpse of four German Focke-Wulfz (biplanes). Wind whizzed past the plane's fuselage as Marinelli maneuvered the Piper into a narrow pathway through the stream bed below the surrounding trees. Yet, as quickly as they had approached, the German planes disappeared.

In the following days, Bourke-White photographed human dramas unfolding in foxholes and Army field hospitals. She lived every moment of her remarkable stories and photographs. Bourke-White endured enemy fire, mud, and cold, and she ate C rations. When her assignment was completed, she returned to New York and wrote *Purple Heart Valley*, a combat chronicle of the war in Italy.

In 1944, with the book completed, she returned to the front lines, accompanying General George S. Patton's Third Army. No experience prepared her

Margaret Bourke-White photographed many events throughout Europe during World War II. Here she is shown photographing a downed German airplane.

for the horrors of the German concentration camps. "Buchenwald was more than the mind could grasp," she later wrote. "I [had] to work with a veil over my mind."[6]

Bourke-White had covered many tough stories, but being a woman was a distinct disadvantage when it came to going on air missions over Germany. Male correspondents were readily given okays. She tried, but never received such permission.

After V-E Day (Victory in Europe) in 1945 Bourke-White went to Essen, Germany, to do a story on the huge Krupp munitions factories. She interviewed and photographed Alfred Krupp, asking him about the forced labor used in his war plants. He was haughty, denying knowledge of any atrocities.[7] Upon her return home, Bourke-White wrote *Dear Fatherland, Rest Quietly.* The U.S. Treasury used this book at the Nuremberg trials.

Bourke-White went to India in 1946 to interview Mohandas Gandhi. Her intimate talks and photos with Gandhi were extraordinary. She remained in the country for two years, witnessing India's independence in 1948.

Later in 1950, when the North Korean forces invaded South Korea, Bourke-White asked to cover the Korean people. She spent months with the guerillas, photographing the people and writing their stories.

Possibly her greatest challenge came in Tokyo in 1950 when she felt a dull ache in her left leg while walking upstairs.[8] When the pain refused to disappear, she returned home. Her malady was identified as Parkinson's, an incurable disease affecting the brain's motor centers that coordinate voluntary movement.

For nineteen years Bourke-White fought back. She walked and danced, and she worked her hands—crushing countless paper balls to try to keep the muscles mobile. Despite two major brain surgeries, the disease continued its ill-fated course.

In 1969 actress Teresa Wright portrayed Bourke-White in the television play *The Margaret Bourke-White Story*. With her usual exacting eye Bourke-White was behind the camera, showing Wright how the crippling disease affected its sufferers. Between scenes she resumed her therapy, tossing a rubber ball.[9]

Before her death on August 27, 1971, Bourke-White asked for, and received, the *Life* assignment to cover the Moon. Her fondest wish was that science would advance enough to enable her to carry out this assignment—Margaret Bourke-White's photo essay of the moon.[10] After all, she had covered most everything else.

Ludmilla "Lou" Ferenz

6

Ludmilla "Lou" Ferenz
(1921–)

Already the tropical heat rose from the isolated sandy beaches of Kwajalein, in the Marshall Islands of the South Pacific. Lieutenant "Lou" Ferenz, American Army nurse, stood under the camouflaged wing of the C-47 airplane. She was preparing her patients for the nine-hour flight eastward across the Pacific Ocean to Hawaii.

"Soon we'll be airborne," she said, smiling to one of the wounded men lying on a stretcher.[1] His khaki uniform was caked with dried mud and stained with blood. For him and the other thirty-eight wounded soldiers nearby, their participation in World War II was over.

Suddenly the morning air came alive with the deep-throated roar of two powerful engines. Sand whirled between the transport's huge rubber tires. "Let's get them on board," she called to two stretcher-bearers, "And take it easy with them."[2] Ferenz was the medical officer in charge of all the patients. Two medical sergeants assisted her with the less seriously injured. They could also administer oxygen.

Just before the plane's metal door swung shut, a flight surgeon jumped aboard for a last-minute check. From a clipboard he pointed out the individual injuries. "Here's what you have today, Lieutenant. Three shell-shock cases (hysterical conditions appearing in soldiers exposed to extreme warfare), five spinal cord injuries, and the rest multiple wounds. Today's flight is straight through to the Pacific-based hospital in Pearl Harbor. And as soon as you're in the air better give No. 10 some plasma. He's lost a lot of blood."[3]

"Yes, sir."

"Are you ready, Lieutenant?" the pilot asked.

Lou Ferenz nodded, checking to be sure that all her patients were strapped in. Then the flight surgeon was gone and a lumbering surge was felt. The C-47 airplane pulled up, rising above the tiny Marshall Island base.

At 7,000 feet the plane leveled. Ferenz unstrapped her seat belt and immediately prepared plasma for No. 10. As she did so she caught sight of a wounded sailor across the aisle. He was suffering from shell shock.

"How are you doing," she asked him.

His fingers squeezed her hand. "I can't stand being tied in. Undo me!"

"The straps are for your own safety. We have a long way to go. And you never know about the weather. I'll come back and give you a mild sedative. Help you to relax." Ferenz knew from his medical chart that he was frightened and very sick. She would have to keep a close watch on him.[4]

The interior of the plane began to cool off, and she snuggled into her flight jacket. Making her way down the aisle she checked the patients' vital signs, tucked in blankets around the sleeping, and gave a cheerful word to those awake. When she reached the shell-shocked sailor she pulled a small packet of morphine (a painkiller) out of her pocket.

If Ferenz had not been charged with caring for her mangled patients, she would have cried. The terrible destruction of so many young men was almost overpowering. But this was her duty. She had joined the Army Nurse Corps for this very purpose.

All her life she had wanted to be a pilot. But her father was against this idea. Flying, nevertheless, was what got her into nursing. Lou Ferenz was born on November 2, 1921, in Yonkers, New York. Her father, Michael Ferenz, owned a grocery store. Both he and her mother, Maria Ferenz, came from the Czech Republic. Together, they raised eleven children—six boys and five girls.

In 1940 Ludmilla "Lou" Ferenz graduated from high school. Since she could not fly she yearned to be a flight attendant. But to be accepted by an airline, a woman had to be a registered nurse. She asked her father about going to college. But in his old country manner he said "no." Women either went to work after high school or they married.[5]

Lou's mother had passed away, so it was Lou's aunt who came forward and offered to pay her college tuition. When her father heard about this, his pride would not allow handouts. "No, Lou could go to nursing school." He would pay for it.[6]

Ferenz entered St. Luke's Hospital in New York. She trained in all phases of nursing, but most enjoyed the surgical aspects. While she was in training, Pearl Harbor was bombed. The following day—December 8, 1941—America declared war on Japan. The government also froze nurses from becoming flight attendants because their services were vital to the war effort.

When Ferenz graduated from St. Luke's, instead of joining United Airlines, she joined the U.S. Army Nurse Corps. Trained nurses were a part of the military forces involved in World War I. In the United States many were drawn from the Red Cross. With World War II, nurses made more progress in military rank and responsibilities commensurate with their training and abilities.[7]

In the early 1940s flight nursing was a recent advancement. The idea of removing the wounded from combat zones by airplane had only recently been developed. The creator of the Air Evacuation

Service was air surgeon for Army Air Forces, Brigadier General David N. W. Grant.

Pilots were trained to fly at levels where smooth air prevailed to give the evacuated wounded as comfortable a flight as possible. The less seriously wounded were placed toward the rear of the airplane's cabin, where the side-to-side movement (yaw) of the plane was the greatest. The more serious cases rested far forward.

The pilot and the flight nurse worked as a team, conferring on acceptable flying altitudes. For instance if a patient with a lung injury was aboard, the pilot would fly at less than 10,000 feet for better oxygen. During World War II, medical evacuation was saving untold numbers of lives. The Army believed that bringing in nurses was uplifting to the wounded as well as relieving medics for more dangerous duties. Flight nursing involved a new aspect of medical training.

Ferenz and the other nurses who entered the Army program were given a three-month general refresher course, including care for the war wounded. They were also schooled in military customs and problems peculiar to air evacuation. Dosage of narcotics at high altitudes are not the same as at sea level. Limited oxygen was often given to air-evacuated patients. How to load a litter on and off the airplane as well as a tough military ground course were also included in their schooling.[8]

The day the coveted gold wings were pinned on Ferenz's uniform, she knew she had chosen the right career. Ferenz arrived in Hawaii in August 1944. She was assigned to "island hop" from Manila in the Philippines back to Pearl Harbor, Hawaii, picking up the seriously wounded from various island locations.

On this particular trip, as the medical transport's twin engines hummed on, Ferenz's thoughts returned to her patients and the responsibility she carried as a flight nurse. This thinking got her back on her feet to make patient rounds again.[9] The two medical sergeants were in the rear of the plane talking to several of the less seriously wounded. Ferenz checked No. 10, touching his forehead and offering an encouraging smile.[10]

There was a sudden clamor near the door of the airplane. Ferenz moved closer. Somehow one of the shell-shocked sailors had gotten out of his litter (the transport's stretcher). His body was pressed against the door.

"I can't take it any longer," he was crying. "I'm going to jump."

"What's the trouble young man?" Ferenz spoke quietly.

"I'm going to jump! I want to die."

"What will that solve?"

"Open that door while we are in the air," said one of the sergeants, "and you take some of us with you."

Ferenz reached out her hand. "Come on. We can talk this out."

Lou Ferenz worked as a flight nurse during World War II, making island hops, and tending the wounded.

"No, let me jump. I can't take the nightmares anymore."

"Leave him alone," said Ferenz, as two sergeants moved to grab him. "Let him jump." She cringed at what she was saying. A nurse agreeing with a sick patient. Yet reverse psychology was all she could think of. Then she stretched her hand out once again.

Once more the sailor twisted the door handle.

"I'm here with you all the way," she said calmly.

Suddenly the young sailor crumbled to the cabin floor, sobbing and shaking. She dropped to her knees, cradling him in her arms until he fell asleep.[11]

"The very first element for having control over others is, of course, to have control over oneself. If I cannot take charge of myself I cannot take charge of others,"[12] Florence Nightingale had written. (Nightingale is regarded as the founder of modern methods of nursing.) Ferenz had stood the challenge. Sometime later the pilot announced Pearl Harbor was coming into view.

Ferenz continued to make the island hops, tending the wounded, throughout the war. On September 2, 1945, the Japanese surrendered. Major General Jonathan Wainwright, who had been a captive since April 1942, was returned to the United States. Ferenz's squadron ferried him and other prisoners of war out of Japan. Ferenz received the Asian-Pacific Medal, as well as Good Conduct and Unit Citation ribbons.

After the war ended Ferenz went home and married Captain Charles Waldrop. They had one son, named Charles Jeffrey Waldrop. In 1949 the family moved to California. The Korean War was starting to take shape. Ferenz's husband was reactivated. In 1957 their marriage ended in divorce. Ferenz began to think about returning to private nursing. She went to work in the office of Dr. Mayo Smith in Whittier, California. Ferenz stayed at this job for twenty years.

After retirement she became a Red Cross volunteer in charge of a community blood mobile. Remarrying, she joined her new husband, Banner Rice, in taking an active part in the Civil Air Patrol. (This was a civilian auxiliary of the United States Air Force that performed search and rescue work.)

Flight nursing began during World War II to evacuate the seriously injured to base hospitals more quickly. Extraordinary advances have since been made, including the use of helicopters dropping into battle to retrieve the wounded. Through it all, however, the thirst for saving lives of the sick, wounded, and injured remains constant. With dedicated and compassionate nurses such as Lou Ferenz this tradition is assured.

Marguerite Higgins

7

Marguerite Higgins
(1920–1966)

During the summer of 1950 Marguerite Higgins's eyewitness coverage of the Korean War was front-page news. "Seoul's Fall by a Reporter Who Escaped" captured page one of the *New York Herald Tribune*, as did "With the United States Marines at Inchon, Korea." Her writing, while praised, did not come about without courage and personal risk:

> We were trapped. The Han River lay between us and safety to the south, and the only bridge had been dynamited. We turned our jeep back to the Korean Military Advisory Group headquarters. There in the darkness, punctuated by shell bursts, the fifty-nine men of Colonel Wright's staff were slowly gathering.

War correspondent Marguerite Higgins, twenty-nine, was facing one of the most awesome events of her life.

The North Korean communist troops were advancing. Seoul, the capital of South Korea, would soon fall to the communists. In blowing up the bridge, the South Korean troops destroyed the only means of escape, leaving behind many of their own troops and the American detachment.

In her book *War in Korea,* Higgins said that she was confident that they would get over the river, even if they had to swim. Her initial concerns were for her three correspondents and for getting her story out.[1]

Sensing her gloom, Colonel Sterling Wright offered, "Look, stick by this radio truck and we'll try to sent out a message for you if you keep it short."[2]

Higgins found her typewriter and set it on the front of the Jeep. As streams of retreating soldiers passed the American convoy, Higgins later wrote in her book, the troops could not help gaping at the woman typing on the hood of a Jeep. Artillery began zeroing in as she completed the last part of her story. Obviously, if the Americans did not want to be captured, they would have to abandon their equipment and swim across the river.

At the river's edge, South Korean soldiers fired at boatmen. They were trying to force the boatmen to come to the soldiers' rescue. Other soldiers jumped aboard any available craft, often swamping the tiny boats. Holding back the rush of South Koreans by rifle point, the band of Americans finally made it safely across the river.

Following a muddy path the Americans were joined by a rain-soaked column of tattered soldiers, old men, diplomats, women, and children. After about fours hours a Jeep appeared, picking up Higgins and several officers.

Marguerite Higgins was born in Hong Kong, China, on September 3, 1920. Her father had taken a job with the Pacific Mail Steamship Company and was assigned to Hong Kong as assistant freight manager. "Maggie" learned Chinese from her amah (Chinese nursemaid), formal French from her mother, and spoken French from her American father, Lawrence Daniel Higgins. An American flyer, Lawrence had served with the famous Lafayette Escadrille during World War I. Afterward he took a French bride, returned to his hometown of Oakland, California, and became assistant manager for the Pacific Mail Steamship Company.

While still a young child, Marguerite and her mother traveled back and forth to France to visit relatives. When Marguerite reached school age she began her formal education in California. The family settled once again in the Oakland foothills. In exchange for Marguerite's scholarship at the exclusive Anna Head School, Mrs. Higgins taught French. Marguerite was an excellent student, who also took ballet and violin lessons, learned French cooking, read the works of Ernest Hemingway, and played basketball.

In 1937 Marguerite entered the University of California at Berkeley. Despite high grades, she was not accepted into the Alpha Phi sorority. Perhaps it was because of her parents. Her mother was typically French, unschooled in the prim Victorian heritage of Americans.

"As much as I personally liked Maggie's parents, I could see that they were different. Mrs. Higgins just wasn't proper enough," said Phoebe True, Marguerite's childhood friend.

Other friends visiting the Higgins's house recalled overhearing violent arguments between Maggie's parents.[3] Higgins joined Gamma Phi Beta instead. "[She] was the ideal sorority girl—pretty, cheerful, a good student, and popular."[4]

As a freshman Higgins's joined the staff of the university newspaper. The *Daily Californian*, published entirely by students, stressed ethics and strong journalism techniques. It was considered a leading university paper. In 1940, as a senior, Higgins was appointed night editor of the paper. She wanted to become editor, but was passed over. One year later she graduated *cum laude* with a bachelor's degree in letters and science.[5]

"I had given myself just one year in which to land a newspaper job. A career in journalism symbolized the epitome of excitement and adventure."[6] Her goal was to work in New York

City. If this proved impossible, she would head back to California and secure a teaching job.

With her scrapbook of clippings from the *Daily Californian* she approached the *New York Herald Tribune*'s editor, stating, "I'm looking for a job."

Instead of brushing her off, L. L. Engelking answered, "What with the draft taking so many of the staff, we may have to fill in with a few women. Come back in a month. There may be an opening."[7]

Despite reluctance to accept women, ten months later, Higgins wrangled her way into the Columbia University Graduate School of Journalism. The following June she became the Columbia University correspondent for the *New York Herald Tribune* and was officially put on the payroll:

> I was so violently intent on becoming a war correspondent there was no time or emotion left over for humility or self-doubt. . . . Getting overseas was something I felt too strongly about to be prepared to stand politely in line and wait my turn.[8]

She badgered every accessible boss at the paper to let her go overseas. As it turned out she asked Helen Rogers Reid, wife of the *Tribune* owner.

In February 1945 she walked into the Hotel Scribe, Paris, as a fully accredited war correspondent. In Paris she wrote two to three stories a day, sometimes filing 3,000 words and working up to 20 hours a day.

Having served two and a half years in Europe, Higgins was assigned to the Far East after the war:

> My editors had sound reasoning for the transfer. . . . Freshness of viewpoint is extraordinarily important to a journalist. . . . Secondly . . . our Moscow correspondent . . . wanted to come to Berlin and his standing in the New York office was higher than mine.[9]

Still the Orient proved to be the making of Marguerite Higgins:

> Why did I ever get myself into this? . . . one of the times I felt this reaction most strongly was in the process of getting the story which I think was the best I wrote out of Korea. It was the eyewitness account of the fabulous amphibious assault behind the North Korean enemy lines at Inchon Harbor.[10]

Debating with herself as to whether or not she would accompany the assault troops, a naval officer unexpectedly announced that no women reporters would be permitted on any phase of the operation. Higgins, nevertheless, requested permission, reasoning that her newspaper's competitive position would be undermined by such a ban. On this basis permission was granted.[11]

The steel-sided landing craft of the Fifth Marine Regiment wove its way toward the sea wall, dodging bright orange and blue tracer bullets. One correspondent said that he'd had enough and was going back to the ship.

Higgins made a decision:

> [I]f I'd turned back then, I would have had a
> hard time facing not only the Marines who
> hit the beaches but the other correspondents,
> and above all the various officials with whom
> I'd raised such cain in order to be allowed on
> the landing in the first place.[12]

Her driving force to get the story, and get it first, had always caused considerable backlash among her peers. "The way to treat Higgins is to get tough," said one correspondent.[13] Another journalist wrote a scathing novel about a woman reporter who broke all the rules. The press assumed it was Higgins.

Marguerite Higgins believed women correspondents should be allowed at war fronts. "Certainly unusual disadvantages face a woman war correspondent. One is the fact that since her presence is highly unusual anything she does, good or bad, is bound to be exaggerated and talked about."[14]

And talked about she was. She wrote an article in *Time* magazine criticizing U.S. occupational forces in Germany as "brawling, raucous boors who whistle and shout '*Kommen hier Sie*'" from street corners "at every passing fraulein." The *Army Times* rebuffed Higgins with an article "How To Write Out of Your Hat," suggesting that she exaggerated certain events.[15]

Higgins remained in the Korean war zone for twenty-three months. This reporting feat earned her the Pulitzer Prize for international reporting—a first for a woman.

Marguerite Higgins believed women correspondents should be allowed at war fronts. Here, she interviews Brigadier General John S. Bradley near the front lines in Korea in 1951.

Her first marriage to Stanley Noone in 1942 ended in divorce in 1948. In 1952, after Korea, Higgins married Lieutenant General William Hall, former director of U.S. Intelligence in Berlin. The couple had two children. Her first child, a premature baby girl, lived only a few days. Over the years, Higgins's desire to report news-breaking stories to the world had not diminished.

When the war in Vietnam broke out, Higgins traveled back to Southeast Asia. There, she interviewed the outspoken Madame Nhu, sister-in-law of the president of Vietnam. Nhu lived in the presidential palace and was feared by her compatriots. During their talk Nhu told Higgins, "Power is wonderful!"[16] Earlier Higgins was told how Nhu had pushed the "family laws" through the Vietnamese legislature.[17]

Higgins wrote six books, including *Our Vietnam Nightmare* in 1965. She also sold magazine articles and became a nationally syndicated columnist for *Newsday*. Higgins interviewed many leading figures of the day, including Nikita Khrushchev, Charles de Gaulle, Jawaharal Nehru, Chiang Kai-shek, the Shah of Iran, as well as Presidents Eisenhower, Truman, and Johnson.

During Higgins's tenth visit to Vietnam she acquired a rare tropical disease called leishmaniasis. She entered Walter Reed Hospital for treatment, but died several months later. Marguerite Higgins was a woman who insisted upon making men's rules work for her. She forged a path for other women journalists to follow.

Mary Walsh

8

Mary Walsh
(1950–)

In a sunlit ceremony that mixed tears, smiles, and speeches, the Vietnam Women's Memorial in Washington, D.C., was unveiled on November 11, 1993. Eleven women veterans held hands in a semicircle around the monument. It was shrouded by a red, white, and blue parachute. Other veterans quietly stood nearby while a warm autumn breeze rustled the golden leaves of overhanging trees. The musical score from the film *Dances with Wolves* enhanced the sobering background.

As the music stopped each of the women in the semicircle clutched the nylon cover and pulled it away to reveal a life-sized bronze work. The statue, completed by sculptor Glenna Goodacre of New Mexico earlier in 1993, depicted an Army nurse sitting on a stack of sandbags holding a wounded male soldier. A second woman looks skyward, anticipating the arrival of a MEDIVAC helicopter. A third kneels, holding a helmet and looking at the ground.

The symbolic statue commemorated approximately eleven thousand American military women who were stationed in Vietnam during the war—most of them as nurses, doctors, and physical therapists. Eight military women who died during the Vietnam War are recognized on the Vietnam Veterans Memorial, nearby in Washington D.C. A total of fifty-three civilian women died in Vietnam. More than a quarter of a million women served during the twelve years of the Vietnam War. Mary Walsh, in her forties, was among the group. She watched the unveiling, half expecting to hear the whirling blades of a MEDIVAC helicopter or the powerful drone of the engines of a C-130 hospital airplane.

In 1967 Mary Walsh had stood on the tarmac at Tan Son Nhut airport, which was on the outskirts of Saigon, South Vietnam. A young U.S. Army physical therapist, she waited to airlift her patient, a critically wounded burn victim, to Brook General Hospital in Fort Sam Houston, Texas. The injured soldier had miraculously been airlifted from the battlefield and saved in a field hospital. His long-term rehabilitation would take place back in the United States.

Touching the ground, the airplane's huge rear cavern opened. Corpsmen carried forty more stretcher patients up the plane's ramp. The other wounded would be cared for by Army nurses and medical corpsmen. The less serious would be flown on to hospitals near their hometowns. In all, the flight from Vietnam to Brook General in Texas would take over fifteen hours. During this flight Walsh's skill and training would be tested.

Mary Walsh was born in 1950 in Glendale, California, to Joseph and Florence Walsh. She had three brothers and one sister—all raised in the Roman Catholic religion. Walsh attended Holy Family elementary school and high school.

Mary's brother, Dave Walsh, was handicapped and wheelchair-bound due to meningitis. (Meningitis is a swelling of the brain.) As a child Mary helped care for him. She also played soldiers with her older brother, John. At age ten she joined the California Rangers Drill Team. "It was military style too," she recalled.[1]

A few years later John Walsh enlisted in the Navy. Mary soon enrolled at Glendale College but a different future was in store:

> One day I was walking up Brand Boulevard, thinking about what I wanted to do and I passed an Army recruiting office. I was eighteen. I went in to inquire about enlisting. The Army recruiter came to my house to discuss enlistment. My mother was all for it, but my father would have no part of it.[2]

To join the military service during the 1960s women had to be eighteen years old, have both parents' consent, be a high school graduate, and have a clean legal record. "I did," said Mary, who convinced her father and was soon enlisted in the Women's Army Corps.[3]

She took basic training at Fort McClellan in Alabama. From there she was sent to Fort Sam Houston, Texas, location of the U.S. Army Medical Field Service School. Walsh studied field medical training, child birth, and physical therapy. She graduated as private first class physical therapist Specialist.

Although Fort Sam Houston was barely one hundred years old, it was part of a military tradition in San Antonio. The history stretched back to 1718, when Mexican troops were assigned to a garrison in the Mission San Antonio de Balero, which later became the Alamo. Fort Sam Houston had also become a burn specialty facility—the largest in the world. The Vietnam War produced the most critically wounded soldiers ever to survive evacuation to a mainland hospital.

According to Major General Spurgeon Neel, former U.S. Army Deputy Surgeon General, "It was a 'dirty war.'" Yet, helicopters were able to evacuate most casualties to medical facilities before a serious wound became worse. There were particularly no conditions under which the injured were denied timely evacuation; all were surmounted by the capabilities of the air ambulances and the skill of their crews.[4]

Many of the more seriously wounded soldiers were multiple amputees and severely burned patients. Their recovery required long and arduous treatments. Swift and efficient MEDIVAC helicopters transported the wounded from firefights to hospitals where doctors and nurses gave emergency medical treatment.

Physical therapists, occupational therapists, and dieticians had all been developed during World War I (1914–1918). Before that time physical therapy was relatively unknown. Emma Lou Vogel perfected physical therapy while developing the Army's school in the early 1900s. The world wars created large numbers of young, seriously handicapped persons. The result was the development of physical therapy as a specialized medical service. By the time war in Vietnam occurred, physical therapists were highly skilled. Their treatment helped relieve pain, improved strength and mobility, and increased breathing capacity and muscular coordination.

The means most commonly used included heat, massage, exercise, and functional training. Walsh's work also included hydrotherapy. "During one day I would have five whirlpools going at once," she said. "Three were sterile whirlpools."[5] Exercise in whirlpool baths proved a big help with healing sore or damaged muscles. The whirlpool provided both warmth and massage. Open-wound treatment was also given in sterile whirlpool baths. "Lanolin was sometimes applied over scars and covered with moist heat," she said.[6]

Walsh also used heat treatments with the aid of ultra sound. These treatments stimulated circulation and relieved pain in the affected area. Massage was used primarily to aid circulation and relieve local pain or muscle spasm.

Waterbeds were also developed and used in the hospital, noted Walsh. The beds' biggest attribute was that patients did not suffer from bed sores—so common in lengthy bed recoveries.

Physical therapy helped rehabilitate hundreds of war-injured patients, bringing back critical muscle use and assisting the permanently injured to live more comfortable and productive lives—often despite the persistence of a medical problem.

When her three-year tour was up, Walsh re-enlisted for four years. This time she was sent to the Army photography school in Monmouth, New Jersey. After completion she was assigned to Fort Huachuca, Arizona, working in the photography section. She was then sent back to work in physical therapy. Two and a half years later Staff Sergeant Mary Walsh took an early discharge.

She returned to Glendale College, receiving an associate's degree in psychology. Then she entered California State University in Los Angeles and earned her bachelor degree in sociology. She next received her master's degree in Post-Traumatic

Staff Sergeant Mary Walsh spent some time at Fort Huachuca, Arizona, working in the Army photography lab. Here, she is pictured at age twenty-one.

Stress Disorder (PSTD)—Social Psychology Specialist. Post-Tramatic Stress Disorder is now widely acknowledged as "normal reactions to abnormal situations."

Mary Walsh worked at various civilian jobs. For instance, she worked for the Internal Revenue Service (IRS) as a tax examiner, and also as a substitute teacher in the Glendale School District at both the junior and senior high school levels. Mary Walsh is currently studying for her doctorate degree in psychology.

Since the Vietnam War, Walsh has been active in the Vietnam Veterans of America (VVA). This group is the only congressionally chartered Vietnam-era veterans' organization. The group recognizes the full conflict from its beginning on January 1, 1959, to its truce on April 30, 1975. From the inception of the Vietnam Women's Memorial Statue, Mary Walsh helped to raise funds and to promote the integrity and value of all women who served during the Vietnam War.

Perhaps Walsh's greatest achievements came from those she treated. During the Vietnam Women's Memorial event in 1993, she was approached by a smiling wheelchair-bound veteran, a former patient. "I wanted to find you," he said, stretching out his right arm. "To show you I can use my arm again."[7]

Because of Mary Walsh and the thousands of other medical personnel, hospital mortality rates during the Vietnam War were less than any other war. Major General Neel found that between January 1965 and December 1970, there were 133,447 wounded admitted to medical treatment facilities in Vietnam. And of these, 97,659 were sent to hospitals. Because of quicker and more advanced medical treatment, the mortality rate was nearly half that of World War II.[8]

Megan C. Jans

9

Megan C. Jans
(1952–)

On the morning of August 2, 1990, Iraqi tanks and troops swept across the Iraqi border into its southern neighbor, the small oil-rich nation of Kuwait. This invasion by Iraqi President Saddam Hussein's enormous army began a confrontation that threatened the future of the entire Middle East. The U.S. Administration responded to the invasion by condemning Iraq and calling for immediate withdrawal of Iraqi forces. Jordan and Yemen favored Iraq.[1] Ignoring world censure, Hussein's army pressed onward. By noon of the same day 150,000 Iraqi troops occupied Kuwait City, Kuwait's capital.

Ten days later in Weisbaden, Germany, Major Megan Jans was on her way to meet a friend to play tennis. "As I drove by U.S. Army headquarters I noticed a lot of action. I was surprised. The base was usually quiet on Sunday," she recalled.[2] Jans learned that an attack battalion would leave for Sardinia, Italy, in three days. Her first reaction to the news was, "I couldn't believe it!"[3]

Jans was the executive officer for Task Force Warrior, the brigade's assault and medium lift battalion that had been performing missions throughout Germany, Turkey, France, Belgium, Italy, and Greece. With the Iraqi forces on the move, Jans's battalion was about to be deployed to the Persian Gulf as part of Operation Desert Storm.

The Persian Gulf seemed like a million miles from where Megan Jans had grown up. As a youngster in Chicago, Illinois, the closest she had gotten to flying was an adventurous game she played with her brother. "We pinned towels to our shoulders. From the top step of our front porch we would see how many steps we could jump. I'd jump as far as I could and then yell 'Super Girl.'" The game lasted until her brother missed a step and broke his ankle and "Mom called 'no go.'"[4]

Megan Jans was born in 1952. She is the daughter of Robert Burns Jans, a dentist, and Marguerite Chenal Jans, a homemaker. Megan attended Catholic schools, taking part in basketball and intramural sports. After high school graduation she enrolled in Fairfield Convent College in Connecticut and received her bachelor's degree in political science.

Jans thought about what she could do to guarantee a paycheck and considered a military career. "I asked the Army recruiter about enlisting. 'You can pick the job that you have qualifications for and want to do,' he said. If I opted for officer's training then I could not."[5]

Jans enlisted in the Army and took basic training at Fort Jackson in Columbia, South Carolina. After completing Army basic training, with the intervention of her father, she was then routed to women's officer's basic training at Fort McClellan in Alabama.

In 1976 the little "Super Girl" who leaped over steps began flight training at Fort Rucker in Dothan, Alabama. First there was ground school; then she was behind the instruments of a Hughes two-seater training helicopter:

> It was such a whole new perspective. . . .
> There were no doors, and you could feel the
> sensation of being in the air, currents of wind
> all around and the sun coming in on all sides.
> Five hundred feet up you could see the corn
> fields, trees, and cows in the field. You felt
> how a bird must feel.[6]

After graduation in December 1976 Jans completed the Aviation Maintenance Officers' Course at Fort Eustis, Virginia. She was prepared for her first assignment as a maintenance test pilot at a U.S. base in Frankfurt, Germany. Proudly wearing the rank of lieutenant, she served as the aviation maintenance officer for the flight detachment of the 32nd Signal Battalion.

Jans's job as test pilot involved flights on the UH-1H Huey helicopter and the OH-58A Kiowa, a four-seater observation helicopter. Her work began with an extensive ground check, which was followed by a final air check that tested how the aircraft reacted system by system.

All military women received a giant step forward on September 12, 1979. This was when Jans was pilot in command for the Army's first all-female flight crew. The crew flew a Huey helicopter in support of the NATO exercise REFORGER. "When we landed and the three women got out a group of guys standing nearby couldn't believe we had flown the helicopter by ourselves. 'You really did fly it in?' they asked."[7]

Four years later Megan Jans returned to the United States as a captain, assigned to Davidson Aviation Command Airfield at Fort Belvoir, Virginia:

> This command is considered most prestigious . . . in that missions are routinely flown in support of Congress, the Departments of Defense and State as well as in support of the Army's senior leadership.[8]

Once again Jans held pilot in command status for all special missions. She also served as pilot for medical evacuation missions throughout the National Capital Region. Her Army responsibilities increased as she became branch leader, serving as the brigade's adjutant (personal manager to the brigade—twelve thousand people) for fifteen Huey aircraft and thirty-five personnel.

In 1980 her next assignment, in Seoul, South Korea, was as assistant logistics officer. As pilot in command she flew exercise missions along the border between South and North Korea. Her job was scouting for sites suitable to land helicopters that would assist ground defenses in case of attack. Her thirteen-month tour of duty also included exercises with the Korean army. As a female pilot, Jans proved to be somewhat novel to Korean soldiers, whose army had no women.

Jans first ground assignment came as protocol officer for the Military District of Washington, D.C. This included protocol functions for all joint and Army military ceremonies involving the White House, Congress, Departments of Defense and State, Office of the Chairman of the Joint Chiefs, Army Secretariat, and Army Chief of Staff. "President Ronald Reagan liked military ceremony," said Jans. "During my protocol assignment Prince Charles and Princess Diana were greeted with military honors as were representatives from the African countries."[9]

In 1987 Megan Jans moved to Fort Leaven-worth, Texas, to attend Command and General Staff College. At this one-year graduate school Jans studied Army strategic and operational planning. She then went to Fort Rucker in Dothan, Alabama. After graduating from the three-month course she was rated in the UH-60 Blackhawk helicopter. Her next assignment was with the 12th Aviation Brigade in Weisbaden, Germany.

After another promotion to the rank of major in 1987, Jans was selected as the executive officer for Task Force Warrior. This group was a temporary combination of forces under a single commander in order to carry out a specific mission. Then came the Persian Gulf War. Jans oversaw the preparation and movement of the battalion's personnel from Weisbaden to the ports of Dhahran, Saudia Arabia, and one hundred trucks by air and rail to Livorno, Italy.

During this deployment, Jans led her battalion convoys from Dhahran to a site deep in Iraq along the Euphrates River. She flew several combat missions in Iraq and also flew supplies into Iraq, bringing back Arab aircraft. On redeployment (returning all personnel and equipment) she was the brigade's officer-in-command for marshaling, guarding, and convoying over four hundred vehicles from the brigade's location to the Port of Damman, Saudia Arabia.

Kuwait City was liberated February 27, 1991, and on February 28 coalition attacks against Iraq ended. On April 1 of that year, Jans returned to Germany. She flew two missions in support of the White House: the visit of Vice President Dan Quayle to Czechoslovakia and the visit of President George Bush to London, England, for the economic summit.

Jans returned to United States in 1992 and was assigned to the Total Army Personnel Command in Alexandria, Virginia. There, Jans authored the personnel support plans for the fielding (bringing new equipment to Army users) of the Kiowa

During the Persian Gulf War, Megan Jans was responsible for overseeing the preparation and movement of the battalion's personnel from Germany to Saudi Arabia.

Warrior (an advanced scout helicopter), two Apache attack helicopter battalions, and the retirement of the Mohawk. One year later she was selected to serve on the Army staff in her current position, Army legislative liaison officer to Congress. In this duty Jans reports on aviation and ammunition, and explains where the money allocated to the Army is used. "The Army is on the down size," she said. "And my job is forced integration for aviation. To do things in certain time lines and have enough trained people to justify our actions."[10]

On duty at the Pentagon, Jans was the principal author on the decision brief to the Army Chief of Staff that recommended opening combat aviation to female pilots. This action was implemented on April 29, 1993, by then Defense Secretary Les Aspin.

Jans has served nineteen years in the military. She plans to remain a few more years, hoping to achieve a full rank of colonel. "My civilian friends think I have a pretty exciting life, but everyone in the Army does these things," she said modestly.[11]

Summoning up her accomplishments and her awards one has to differ. Lieutenant Colonel Megan Jans is one of three female aviator lieutenant colonels on active duty in the U.S. Army. Jans is the first female commissioned officer authorized to wear the Master Army Aviator Badge (Army aviators who have been flying over fifteen years and accumulated two thousand hours flight time).

Jans holds the Air Assault Badge for completing a course of repelling by rope out of a helicopter and rigging equipment to be attached to the belly of a helicopter. She received the Bronze Star for going beyond the call of duty during combat; four awards of the Meritorious Service Medal—given for fielding of the Warrior, working as manager, doing work of a colonel, and extraordinary duties. The Air Medal was awarded to Jans for flying combat missions and completing military missions as required.

She received three awards for the Army Commendation Medal for the highest number of points while personal manager of her team in Germany, and putting together the Aviators European Conference; three awards of the Army Achievement Medal for a perfect three-year record in physical fitness; the National Defense Medal for going to war; the Southwest Asia Campaign Medal (two stars for "Desert Storm"—the Persian Gulf War), and four service ribbons. She has also completed over 2,100 hours of accident-free flying.

Jans said she is proudest of her Bronze Star and Air Medal—both given for extraordinary merit during times of combat.

Pamela Davis Dorman

Pamela Davis Dorman

(1952–)

There had been friction between the Middle Eastern nations of Kuwait and Iraq for some time. During July 1990, the tension sharply mounted. Observers of the Middle East noted that Saddam Hussein, president of Iraq, needed money to rebuild the country's economy. Iraq had already occupied two offshore Kuwaiti islands. A limited Iraqi move into Kuwaiti territory was expected, but Iraq's full-scale invasion of Kuwait on August 2, 1990, was something else entirely, and no one outside of Iraq had predicted it.[1]

In August 1990 events occurred that heightened speculation of war. Iraqi tanks invaded Kuwait City. The United Nations (UN) also condemned Iraq's action and imposed a trade embargo on Iraq. The

UN further allowed the use of force to halt ships suspected of trading with Iraq.

At the U.S. Navy base at Camp Pendleton, California, Lieutenant Pamela Davis, Navy chaplain, was also aware of pending war. "I knew our battalion was going. But because of fear or religious discrimination (Iraq is a Muslim nation), no women chaplains were going."[2] Allied preparations moved forward, and shortly thereafter, all the military services agreed to send women chaplains too.

U.S. government concern about the Islamic faith was reported in a military document titled "While We Are Here." It stated, "Respect religious places and practices. Do not photograph mosques . . . respect cultural differences of your Saudi hosts."[3]

The next month, at the Helsinki summit, President George Bush and Soviet Union President Mikhail Gorbachev agreed on a plan to deal with Iraq. On November 29 the UN authorized member states to "use all necessary means" to make Iraq comply with previous resolutions. President Bush sent further messages to the military: "If history teaches us anything, it is that we must resist aggression, or it will destroy our freedoms." Clearly tension was high.[4]

U.S. General Norman Schwarzkopf, the Allied commanding officer, issued a written statement to the Americans: "Our mission here is to deter attack and, if an attack comes, we are to defend."[5]

Davis arrived in Saudia Arabia, the western neighbor of Kuwait and Iraq, in November. "There was a lot of excitement. With tanks and supplies unloading twenty-four hours a day it was obvious a confrontation was expected."[6]

Davis was the first female U.S. Navy chaplain to serve with the marines. She was deployed into the northern combat zone within 35 miles of Kuwait. Davis was assigned chaplain for over 140 officers and 850 enlisted corpsmen of the 1st Supply Battalion and then the 1st Medical and 1st Dental battalions.

Although ordained a Lutheran minister, as chaplain, Davis crossed religious boundaries, administering to all Protestant denominations:

> I had five worship services on a given day. Yet the greatest challenge I had was getting around. There were not enough vehicles so I had to borrow a Jeep, traveling to the Army, Navy, Marine, and Air Force desert camp sites.[7]

On January 17, 1991, Allied air bombardment of Iraq began. Air support came from a coalition of the United States, Britain, France, and several Arab nations. By this time Allied forces had reached a total of 550,000 troops—some 350,000 of which were Americans. On January 30, in a surprise attack, Iraqi forces captured the Saudi border town of Khafji and held it for more than a day.

Davis's duties increased. She performed anointing (prayers for physical healing) for critical and terminal patients. She also conducted church services for the medical staff involved in casualty cases. Davis counseled over sixty Armed Forces personnel within one month, and still found time to form a support group for women Marines:

> As one of very few women in the military serving with the Marines, I began the group. This support group became invaluable for many who felt the need to have a safe place to discuss issues that weighed them personally. I provided the place, the format, the counsel, and follow-up visits in the work spaces during our time in Saudi Arabia. It was in a sense a very small thing. But the encouragement it gave the women with whom I ministered was a very effective witness to our faith and human rights.[8]

Pamela Davis was born December 21, 1952, in La Crescenta, California. She is the daughter of Virginia and James Davis, and has one sister. Pamela attended schools in La Crescenta, California, and graduated from Crescenta Valley High School in 1971:

> Around the time I was in high school I became active in my church. In 1971 the Lutheran Church was not ordaining women. So I thought perhaps I would be a missionary or a social parish worker.[9]

Margaret Ermarth, a Lutheran authority on the subject of ordaining women, had observed, "when the issue is women in the priesthood, in almost every church it has been the clergy who have objected most strenuously."[10]

After high school, Davis enrolled at California Lutheran University, receiving her bachelor's degree in 1975. She then attended Pacific Lutheran Theological Seminary and graduated in 1979. When the Lutheran Church recognized women in 1980, Davis was ordained. She became the first ordained woman pastor in the Atonement Lutheran Church to serve a parish in Las Vegas, Nevada. She was also involved with two parish pre-schools, in Las Vegas and San Diego.

Davis was called upon to teach and act as vice-principal to junior and senior high school students at the Heights Lutheran Schools in Hacienda Heights, California. With two hundred students, Davis taught courses in the Old Testament, the Bible, church history, and world religions. Davis later became interim principal. "Teaching youth and adults is hard work," she said, "but I enjoyed it. I always learn as I study to teach, and learn as I receive from my students."[11]

In 1973 the U.S. Navy accepted the first woman chaplain, Lieutenant Florence Dianna Pohlman. Davis though about joining the naval reserves or enlisting full-time. "There were some big changes going on in my life at that time." In December 1988 she enlisted and was commissioned.

103

Among her other tasks while in Saudi Arabia, Pamela Davis administered the sacraments and provided ministry. Here, Davis is preparing for her return to the United States.

Davis spent eight weeks at Chaplain Basic School in Newport, Rhode Island. There, she received officer indoctrination courses, how to wear the uniform, military bearing, military history, and the military way. Each military chaplain also had to be endorsed by his or her church body in order to receive a commission as a chaplain. The commission can be withdrawn at any time for disciplinary reasons or at the bishop's discretion. After graduation Davis was assigned to the 1st Field Support Group at Camp Pendleton. As a military chaplain Davis represented her church body and her bishop. "I continually served as a reminder to all that I was first a Lutheran pastor who wore a Navy uniform."[12]

During deployment in Saudi Arabia, Pamela administered the sacraments, provided ministry, and carried out a variety of related tasks. She held Eucharist services and weekly worship. Other duties occupied Davis as well. She maintained supervision over her enlisted staff, managed a well-organized ministry and office, and acted as morale officer for Kilo Company.

In presenting Pamela with the Navy Commendation Medal, Brigadier General J. A. Brabham said:

> She was instrumental, by virtue of her superior dedication, in enhancing the morale and welfare of not only the individuals with whom she made contact, but also with several battalions to which she was assigned, enabling all to complete their assigned missions. Lieutenant Davis's exceptional professionalism,

unfailing good judgement, and extreme devotion to duty and fellow servicemen reflected great credit upon herself and were in keeping with the highest traditions of the United States Naval Service.[13]

Kuwait City was liberated on February 27, 1991. On February 28 President Bush ordered a cease-fire, and hostilities ended. The UN Security Council officially declared an end to the war on April 11, 1991.

During her service years Davis attended area clergy meetings too. She was asked by the bishop to chair the Task Force for Policy, Procedure and Guidelines for Sexual Abuse in the Pacifica Synod. Her significant awards include the Navy Commendation Medal, Navy Unit Commendation ribbon, USN Fleet Marine Force ribbon, National Defense Medal, Southwest Asia Medal, Overseas Service ribbon, and Kuwait Liberation Medal.

Davis returned to the United States after the Kuwaiti liberation. She was discharged from active duty in June 1993. While in Saudia Arabia, Davis met James Dorman, a general surgeon with the U.S. Navy. While Davis said that she never wants to go through a war again, she acknowledged a good result of the Persian Gulf War—meeting, and later marrying, Lieutenant Dorman.

Pamela Davis Dorman and her husband make their home in Salt Lake City, Utah. She is planning to return to her ministry.

Chapter Notes

Chapter 1

1. Rupert Furneaux, *Pictorial History of the American Revolution* (Chicago: J. G. Ferguson Publications, 1973), p. 232.

2. Augusta Stevenson, *Molly Pitcher: Young Patriot* (Indianapolis: Bobbs-Merrill, 1983), p. 183.

3. Ibid., p. 185.

4. Dumas Malone, ed., *Dictionary of American Biography*, Vol. VI, Part 1 (New York: Charles Scribner's Sons, 1933), p. 574.

5. Stevenson, pp. 186–187.

6. Ibid., p. 188.

7. Jan Guitno and Kathleen Thompson, *Molly Pitcher* (Milwaukee, Wis.: Raintree Children's Books, 1987), pp. 28–29.

8. "Colonial Life in America," *World Book Encyclopedia,* Vol. 17 (Chicago, Ill.: Field Enterprise Education Corporation, 1958), p. 8424.

9. Ibid., p. 266.

10. "Molly Pitcher," *Encyclopedia Americana,* Vol. 19 (Danbury, Conn.: Grolier Incorporated, 1991), p. 335.

11. Ibid.

Chapter 2

1. Oscar A. Kinchen, *Women Who Spied for the Blue and the Gray* (New York: Dorrance and Co., 1972), p. 14.

2. Sylvia G. L. Dannett, *She Rode With the Generals* (New York: Thomas Nelson & Sons, 1960), p. 117.

3. Kinchen, p. 15.

4 Harnett T. Kane, *Spies for the Blue and Gray* (Garden City, N.Y.: Doubleday & Co., 1954), p. 12.

5. "The Civil War," *World Book Encyclopedia*, Vol. 4 (Chicago, Ill.: Field Enterprise Education Corp., 1993), p. 624.

6. Kinchen, p. 19.

7. Dannett, p. 139.

8. Amy H. Berger, "Sarah: The Woman Who Fought in the Civil War as a Man," *Woman's World,* June 6, 1989, p. 30.

Chapter 3

1. Susan Raven and Alison Weir, *Women of Achievement* (New York: Harmony Books, 1981), p. 245.

2. Personal letters from Mary Walker (Oswego, N.Y.: Oswego County Historical Society, January 23, 1872).

3. Fred P. Wright, "Dr. Mary Walker: Trousered Civil War Surgeon, Recalled," *The (Oswego, N.Y.) Post Standard,* December 8, 1938, p. 1.

4. Robert McHenry, ed., *Famous American Women* (New York: Dover Publications, 1980), p. 427.

5. Ibid.

6. Wright, p. 1.

7. Ibid., p. 5.

8. Ibid.

9. Ibid.

Chapter 4

1. *Friends of France: The Field Service of the American Ambulance* (Boston: Houghton Mifflin Co., 1916), p. 115.

2. "Gorgas, William Crawford," *World Book Encyclopedia,* Vol. 7 (Chicago, Ill.: Field Enterprise Education Corp., 1958), p. 3066.

3. Edith A. Aynes, *From Nightingale to Eagle* (New York: Prentice-Hall, 1957), p. 38.

4. John Boyd Coates, Jr., *Organization and Administration in World War II* (Washington, D.C.: Office of the Surgeon General, Department of the Army, 1963), p. 180.

5. Doris W. Egge, *A Concise Biography of Florence Aby Blanchfield, ANC* (Maryland: Historical Unit U.S. Army, 1974), pp. 1–3.

6. J. A. Ulio, *War Department, The Adjutant General's Office* (Washington, D.C., June 11, 1945), p. 1.

7. "Citation for Distinguished Service Medal," War Department, June 11, 1945, p. 1.

Chapter 5

1. Margaret Bourke-White, *Portrait of Myself* (New York: Simon and Schuster, 1963), p. 207.

2. Ibid., p. 203.

3. Ibid., p. 30.

4. Ibid.

5. Margaret Bourke-White, *They Call It "Purple Heart Valley"* (New York: Simon and Schuster, 1944), p. 7.

6. Bourke-White, *Portrait of Myself,* p. 259.

7. Ibid., p. 267.

8. Ibid., p. 358.

9. "A Brave Story Retold," *Life,* January 11, 1960, pp. 78–79.

10. Bourke-White, *Portrait of Myself,* p. 383.

Chapter 6

1. Personal interview with Ludmilla "Lou" Ferenz, October 1992.

2. Ibid.
3. Ibid.
4. Ibid.
5. Ibid.
6. Ibid.
7. "Nursing," *Encyclopaedia Britannica* (Chicago, Ill.: Encyclopaedia Britannica, 1980), Vol. 13, pp. 396–397.
8. Personal interview with Ludmilla "Lou" Ferenz, October 1992.
9. Ibid.
10. Ibid.
11. Ibid.
12. Edith A. Aynse, *From Nightingale to Eagle* (New York: Prentice-Hall, 1967), p. 302.

Chapter 7

1. Marguerite Higgins, *War in Korea* (Garden City, N.Y.: Doubleday & Co., 1951), p. 27.
2. Ibid.
3. Antoinette May, *Witness to War* (New York: Beaufort Books, 1983), p. 33.
4. Ibid., p. 35.
5. Ibid., p. 45.
6. Marguerite Higgins, *News I a Singular Thing* (Garden City, N.Y.: Doubleday & Co., 1955), p. 16.
7. Ibid., p. 21.
8. Ibid., p. 40.
9. Ibid., p. 203.
10. Ibid., pp. 210–211.
11. Ibid., pp. 211–212.
12. Ibid.
13. Ibid., p. 204.
14. Ibid., p. 213.
15. "The Press," *Time*, September 24, 1951, p. 76.
16. Marguerite Higgins, *Our Vietnam Nightmare* (New York: Harper and Row, 1965), p. 71.
17. Ibid., p. 61.

Chapter 8

1. Personal Interview with Mary Walsh, December 1993.
2. Ibid.
3. Ibid.
4. Colonel Henry J. Pratt, USAR-Ret., *Heroines of Healing, The Retired Officer* magazine, Vol. XLIX, No. 11, November 1993, p. 30.

5. Personal interview with Mary Walsh, December 1993.

6. Ibid.

7. Personal interview with Mary Walsh, January 1994.

8. Pratt, p. 31.

Chapter 9

1. John King, *The Gulf War* (New York: Dillon Press, 1991), p. 4.

2. Personal interview with Megan Jans, September 1993.

3. Ibid.

4. Personal interview with Megan Jans, December 1993.

5. Ibid.

6. Ibid.

7. Ibid.

8. Ibid.

9. Ibid.

10. Ibid.

11. Personal interview with Megan Jans, April 1994.

Chapter 10

1. John King, *The Gulf War* (New York: Dillon Press, 1991), p. 6.

2. Personal interview with Pamela Davis, January 1994.

3. U.S. Military Instructions, *While We Are Here* (U.S. Navy Publications, Washington D.C.: 1990), p. 1.

4. Ibid.

5. Ibid., p. 2

6. Personal interview with Pamela Davis, January 1994.

7. Ibid.

8. Pamela Davis, *Mobility Information Form, Pastors and Associates in Ministry* (San Diego: Southwest Pacifica Synods, 1993), p. 5.

9. Personal interview with Pamela Davis, January 1994.

10. Emily C. Hewitt and Suzanne R. Hiatt, *Women Priests: Yes or No* (New York: Seabury Press, 1973), p. 98.

11. Davis, p. 6.

12. Personal interview with Pamela Davis, January 1994.

13. J.A. Braham, USMC, Navy Commendation Medal, (Camp Pendleton, California, 1992).

Index